Escaping Poverty

The 4 Categories

Copyright © 2019 by Calvin Dadale Morris

All rights reserved. No part of this book may be reproduced or used in any manner without written permission of the copyright owner.

No part of this book may be stored in a retrieval system, or transmitted electronically, mechanically or by any other means without written permission of the publisher.

Editing by Adriana Morris

All photographs and images by Calvin Dadale Morris

First Edition ISBN 978-1-7339232-1-7

Published by Calvin Dadale Morris

2019

Limit of Liability/Disclaimer of Warranty: Although the author and publisher have made every effort to include helpful information in this book, the author and publisher do not assume and hereby disclaim any liability to any party for any loss, damage, or disruption caused by errors, omissions, advice, ideas or any other part of this book. The author and publisher specifically disclaim any warranty of merchantability.

The information contained in this book is strictly for educational purposes only and may not apply to your personal situation or circumstances. You should consult a professional where appropriate.

Escaping Poverty

The 4 Categories

Written and Published in 2019 by

Calvin Morris

Edited by Adriana Morris

The battle for freedom begins in the hearts and minds of those who desire to be free. Today, the battle begins.

Content

Introduction	1
The Map	13
The Revelation	19
The Light	27
The Power of Positivity	35
A Reliable Truth	45
Believing in You	53
Enough is Enough	65
The Road to Discovery	91
The Big Three	97
The Advantage	119

Preface

Before you even ask me that one, very important question of when I started to believe, let me just tell you the answer. It all began with a connection; a common denominator between he and I. It was our connection and what we had in common that drew me to him and his life. We were both born out of wedlock, Confucius and I — both to teenage mothers. We were born into poverty, raised in single-parent homes and written off by society. Our fathers abandoned us and for selfish reasons, left us alone to suffer the lifelong, scarring effects of poverty. When they left, they left a mountain at our doorsteps. They put a ginormous obstacle between us and success. From the very beginning, we were up against what seemed to be insurmountable odds, but somehow

Confucius found his way to the other side, where he achieved a happy and acceptable life.

The old saying, "It's not where you start, but where you finish" immediately came to mind as I thought about how Confucius took his unconventional beginning and turned it into a remarkable life. It was impressive, because he started at the bottom and worked his way to the top. Not many people can do that, so Confucius deserves recognition.

Confucius once wrote, "The man who moves a mountain begins by carrying away small stones." Words that escaped the pages of my book and found their way into the pages of my life. By moving one stone at a time, I escaped. One stone at a time was more than just a group of words to me. It was a strategy; one that applied to every challenge I faced in life. Those same words can be just as powerful today as they were years ago. Perhaps that's why those words lie at the very foundation of this book.

Preface

What makes this book so valuable is the fact that it provides a strategy that can help you escape poverty, even when an escape is improbable. Every stone can be moved, and this book teaches you how to move them. It guides you past each stone in a step by step, easy to follow way that even a novice can understand. Your mountain cannot stand before you any longer. All you have to do is move it. The time to act is now.

To my mother Mary and my three beautiful children Adriana, Jonathan and Joshua, who all inspired me to be the best person I could be. For your support and encouragement, I am forever grateful. I love you.

INTRODUCTION

According to the U.S. Census Bureau, 39.7 million people are currently living in poverty (in the United States alone); a distressing amount of people to say the least. Even more distressing is the fact that many of them, to no fault of their own, were born in poverty and will more than likely remain in poverty for the rest of their lives. This assumption is based on data from the Center for Poverty Research (UC Davis), which shows a correlation between the amount of time a person spends in poverty and the probability of the person getting out of poverty in his or her lifetime. As the amount of time a person spends in poverty increases, the chances of the person getting out significantly decreases, with only a thirteen percent chance for those who are in poverty for seven or more years.

To some, a thirteen percent chance sounds like no chance at all. It causes many to believe that their destinies are preordained, that their accomplishments are limited and that their dreams are somehow unattainable. The truth is that a thirteen percent chance is at the very least, sufficient enough to show that escaping poverty is possible. Perhaps not only possible, but possible for you.

Abraham Lincoln, Oprah Winfrey, Leonardo DiCaprio, Harry Houdini and so many others were born poor, yet they figured out how to do what very few people could do. They figured out how to escape poverty in a world where escaping poverty was almost impossible. A doctor, lawyer, teacher or whatever you wish to be in life, it will require you to do the same. It will require you to make a nearly impossible escape. I've done it and so can you.

The Location

I spent the first 18 years of my life growing up in a small town in Mississippi, the poorest state in the United States of America. There, I learned some very important life lessons that perhaps, I wouldn't have learned if I'd been born in a less impoverished state. Clarksdale, Mississippi was a fun town, but it lacked the sense of community often found in other small towns across the country.

In the late 80's and early 90's, the city of Clarksdale caught the interest of gang lords in Chicago, who found it to be a convenient place to buy and sell illegal weapons. After transporting weapons from Clarksdale to Chicago, gang lords distributed them into their own communities, where they used them to commit homicides, and to protect territories. Sadly, their plans involved the recruitment of innocent and impressionable children, who eventually became puppets for the gangs of Chicago. For Clarksdale, the big city's influence was too great. Families lost control of their kids and that's when the drama began. An influx of home invasions, property crimes and senseless homicides caused the community to lose its sense of security. As a result, people began to flee the city. Companies soon followed in search of safer and more profitable places to do business, which left an already underemployed community with nowhere to find jobs and eventually, no way to provide for their families.

As more and more people lost their jobs, they began to lose hope in city officials, who they accused of sitting on their hands and doing nothing while the city turned into a shell of what it once was. Without neither the finances to relocate, nor the ability to find jobs, people began to feel stuck and abandoned. Many of them gave up on their dreams and quit trying to better themselves altogether. Unfortunately,

I was one of them. I was one of those people with no hopes, no dreams, no goals and no way out. I was trapped. My hometown turned into my prison.

Dead bodies piled up for what seemed to be every day in my neighborhood. Gunshots filled the night with fear and uncertainty. Many of my friends lost their lives before they even finished high school. Young boys and girls were killed in the early stages of life because they were just like me, stuck and unable to escape the violent city they grew up in. The prison around them had no bars but it was as inescapable as the local penitentiary. All of us felt the pain but none of us knew the way out. Perhaps you feel the same way about where you live and if you do, then I'm here to tell you that you can get out. You can escape, just as I did.

The Prison & the Sentencing

A 6 by 9-foot cell made of solid steel or brick is what most people think of when they hear the word prison, but prisons come in many forms and can be as large as the city around you. They impose limits on a variety of things including how far you can move, what you can do and how much you can obtain. Clarksdale felt very much like a prison to me, but it wasn't the city that was holding me back, it was the poverty that plagued it. In my mind, there's no difference between poverty and prison, except for the fact that going to prison usually involves a more just and fair process.

When a person goes to trial for committing a crime that carries a possible life sentence, it sparks the beginning of a process. The process is designed to ensure that the outcome of the trial is fair and just. With fairness in mind, the legal system allows the accused to have an attorney, along with a jury that ultimately decides his or her level of guilt, and a judge to determine the amount of time he or she will spend in prison. But when a child sits in its mother's belly facing lifelong poverty, there's no process to question the fairness of its circumstances and no legal way to change its fate. There's also no attorney to fight on its behalf, no jury to hear its case and no judge to lower its sentence from life in poverty to only five, ten or even twenty years.

One might argue that comparing life in prison to life in poverty is a nonsensical idea, but in reality, a life in poverty is the same as life in prison and in some cases, even worse. For example, a man serving less than life in prison, serves with the luxury of knowing that one day he may once again be free – a luxury not always afforded a person born into poverty. A man serving life in prison serves only for the life he has, but poverty, on the other hand, imprisons a man for generations well beyond his own. A 6 by 9 ft cell confines the body to a much smaller area than poverty, but the physical, emotional and psychological effects can be very similar.

Are you in some type of prison? If the answer is yes, then the way out is to move the mountain that sits between you and your freedom. To move it, you'll need a better understanding of the things that make up the mountain. These intangible things fall into four categories: Optics, Pressures, Behaviors and Pitfalls.

Optics make up the light or darkness within you. They originate from your heart, soul and mind. You can't escape them, you can't survive without them and you definitely can't ignore them. They are as connected to you as every other part of your body, and like every other part, they can be moved. Pointing them in the right direction is key.

Pressures are those things that sit directly behind your Optics. They often draw out negative emotions, behaviors and responses. Pressures, I like to say, are nothing more than noise. They are louder than their importance and often get in the way of the truth.

Behaviors are those things that share the ingredients of both Pressures and Optics. They can't be changed until your optics are pointing in the right direction and your pressures are of minimal importance. I like to think of behaviors as those things that keep you moving in the right direction, kind of like signs on the side of the road.

Last but not least, the pitfalls, which I consider to be predictable mistakes. They sit directly behind your Behaviors. Sometimes they are big, sometimes they are small, but no matter the size, they can lead right back to poverty. I like to think of them as dangerous decisions that have to be made along the way. All four categories must be understood before you can completely escape poverty.

Explanation of the 4 Categories

The Map

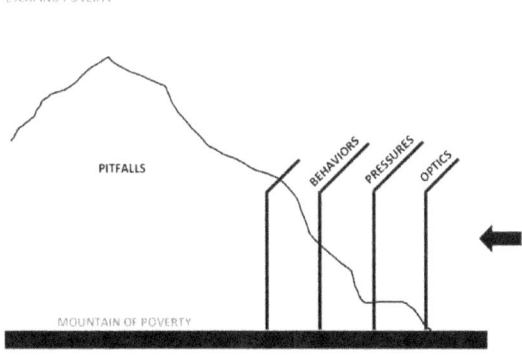

Before the beginning of a long and difficult battle, great minds assemble around what is arguably the most valuable resource they have — a map. William Wallace defeated the English with a map. Alexander the Great crushed the Persians with a map. Caesar marched into Britain with thousands of men, and of course, a map. Every great battle in history has in one way or another, involved a map, which is why I believe you should have a map with you as you battle against poverty.

The greatest battle you've ever faced, will require you to have a map, especially if you plan on winning it. As you plan your escape, every step should be meticulous. Every turn should be thought out, premeditated, deliberate, precise, timely and of course, executed in the right order.

A good map can help you understand where you are, where you need to start and where you need to go. It can also help you understand when to stop, yield, turn or continue on the path you're on. The only way to avoid getting lost, is to check the map as often as possible. This journey may be the toughest you've ever endured, but my hope is that you'll find comfort, courage and confidence in the map that I've provided. Once you understand the map and the four categories, your journey will be much, much easier.

A Path to Freedom

Before I begin to explain the many things that stand between you and the great mountain of poverty, I want to make sure that you understand the four categories in which they fall. The four categories: Optics, Pressures, Behaviors and Pitfalls, all contain their own group of challenges. Take a quick look at the map to see where each category is located.

Together, the four categories form a path to freedom. The path begins within you and extends well beyond the mountain of poverty, where it either ends or continues on for generations to come. If escaping poverty is your goal, then the only path you should be on is the one that begins with you. The path created by the four categories is the only path you should be on, because any other path will lead right back to poverty.

You cannot escape poverty on another person's path; mainly because you haven't gone through what that person has gone through. Somewhere along the path, all of us encounter the pressures of life and when we do, we develop behaviors that either help us avoid pitfalls or cause us to plunge right into them. No matter how much you believe in someone else, you will not escape on that person's path. You must have your own path. The path to your escape must begin and end with you, because you must develop your own, winning behaviors, if you want any chance at all to escape.

The Order

One stone at a time is the smartest way to move a mountain, perhaps that's why I decided to break this book down into four very important categories; categories that I will sometimes refer to as stones. Each of the four categories should be moved one at a time. The fastest way to move them is to move them in the order that they appear in this book. I highly recommend that you address everything in this book one word, one idea, one stone, one category, one page and one day at a time.

Just to be clear; the fastest way to escape poverty is to follow along with this book, stay the course, follow the map and work through each step before moving to the next. I've seen people make their situations worse by trying to do step three before completing step one. Many of them are still trapped in poverty today. You do not want to be like them. They've essentially wasted precious time, energy and resources that they'll never get back.

The order should be followed, especially if you want to get the most out of this book. Skipping ahead, taking shortcuts, wasting resources or calling on people that you're not truly ready to satisfy, is a huge no-no. People will help you when you are ready and willing to help yourself. Don't waste other people's time and energy. When they decide to invest in you, you need to give them a return on their investment. In return for their help, you need to make sure that they are satisfied with the effort that you put in. Stay on the path to freedom and freedom will be your reward.

The Revelation

Before I tell you about the first category, let me ask you a very important question. Do you believe that perception is reality, or do you believe that reality has nothing to do with perception? The reason why I ask is because I need you to know that neither of those things are true, unless they are absolutely true. The only way to permanently escape poverty is to understand that the truth is always true regardless of your perception. Reality is what it is, but perception changes from person to person, which is why the first category, Optics, separates perception from reality. The ability to bend your optics away from reality may change how you see things, but it will never determine what is real and what is not.

This section is called the Revelation because it reveals the one reason why most people remain in poverty. It's because perception and reality coexist on the path to escape, where together they create a paralyzing and often undiscovered illusion. It's the illusion that ultimately hinders your escape.

As you travel along the path created by the four categories, you may find yourself plagued by a series of illusions; illusions that draw out painful and sometimes blinding emotions. For example, the illusion that no one cares about you, may be the very reason why you haven't even attempted to escape. The emotion attached to that kind of illusion can blind you to the point where you can't even see the path before you. On the path lies the truth, but in the face of an illusion the truth is often missed — something I learned during my studies of the Master of Escape, Harry Houdini.

The Houdini Insert

Before I set out to make my own escape, I decided to read about the greatest escape ever attempted, which ultimately helped me understand the power of an illusion. The synopsis, which I've written in my own words, is as follows:

The Torture Cell

One of the greatest escapes of the 20th century occurred in Berlin, Germany in 1912, when American Illusionist, Harry Houdini, escaped what many believed to be the most terrifying contraption the world had ever seen. It was called the Chinese Water Torture Cell. It was a tall, rectangular, air-tight cell filled with water, much like an aquarium, but fortified to make sure nothing got in or out.

Like the brainchild of a mad scientist or an evil villain, the Torture Cell was a man-made monster, capable of bringing the darkness of death into the light, where it could be seen in plain view through its clear, half-inch thick glass and patient, merciless water. It was brought into this world to do one thing and one thing only — and that was to take the art of escape to a place it had never gone before; a place where the stakes were high and where the ultimate end-result of failure was a swift, predictable death.

The Torture Cell was not to be toyed with. It was to be feared, avoided even, unless of course, you were stricken with a death wish, or somehow cursed with a mad man's courage. Only a fool would try to escape it. Yet on September 21st, it sat center stage at the renowned Circus Busch, where Houdini, a magician turned escapologist, was determined to prove he could once again make a way out of no way.

As he hung upside down inside the torture cell, his head was only inches from the floor, his hands were bound, his feet were locked in stocks and his body was completely submerged in water. Around his body was a solid steel cage, which appeared to be exactly what it was; an underwater prison, patiently waiting to punish anyone trapped inside. Dangling inside the cage alone, was the master of escape — clinging to a single breath — staring out at the crowd as blood rushed through his body down to his head. Time was running out and he knew it, yet he seemed unconcerned, perhaps because he wanted so badly to give the crowd what they wanted: an unbelievable, intensely exciting, death-defying escape.

As more and more time ticked off the clock, the crowd began to realize just how improbable an escape really was. More importantly, it forgot something that should never be forgotten; it forgot the fact that things are not always as they seem, especially those things seen by the eyes, heard by the ears and understood by the brain. As the crowd braced itself for the worst, Houdini, with his life on the line, remained confident and calm, while holding what many believed to be his very last breath.

After Houdini stepped out of the Torture Cell, in which he had been trapped for more time than any human could possibly survive, the reaction of the crowd served as proof that the illusion was more powerful than reality. Every single person in the room knew beforehand that Houdini was an illusionist, yet the tension in the room was real. They believed wholeheartedly that he was in danger, and he was, but not quite the danger they believed he was in.

Everything he needed, he had inside the cell with him, just as you have everything you need with you, inside the poverty in which you are trapped. The illusion that you cannot escape is only a product of your own perception, which is why perception is what we'll tackle first in the category called Optics. But before we do, I'd like to share with you this very important fact: the escape from the Torture Cell was perceived by all to be Houdini's greatest escape, when in fact, his greatest escape was his escape from poverty. To know this and not shine light on it would be a disservice to you, because I need you to know that escaping poverty is possible. It may seem like there's no way out, but if I learned nothing else from the Master of Escape, I learned that there's always a way out.

2

Understanding the Optics

The Light

    I don't want to make this sound any more complicated than it already is, but in order to see the path before you, the light that shines within you must be shined in the right direction. That can't happen though, until you take a really close look at who you are, what you stand for and how you see things. One of the biggest mistakes you can make is to try to escape poverty without first adjusting your optics.

    Optics rest at the very core of who you are. They determine how often, or how seldom you will feel happy, sad, inspired, motivated, lonely, humble or even selfish. They are just that important. Optics shine through your heart, eyes, mind, body and soul until every truth about your being is revealed. What you do in the dark, will eventually come to the light, and that light will be powered by your optics.

    Optics shine through so bright that they reveal even the darkest areas of your life. The way you feel is determined by your optics. The way you think is directly related to how you feel. What you believe can be linked all the way back to how you felt when something happened, and how you felt had everything to do with how well you controlled your optics. Drive, confidence, patience, attitude, courage, focus and every other trait known to be present in highly successful people, originated from the light within them.

Perception

Life is good, unless of course, there's a problem with your perception. If that's the case, then you should deal with your perception before trying anything else in this book.

No matter what's going on around you, whether it's gang violence, drug abuse, alcoholism, financial starvation, physical abuse, or the everyday hustle and grind of life, you are in control of how you see the things that are happening to, or as some might say, for you. Good and bad things happen for you when you learn from them. They don't happen to you. Take control of your perception. Now's the time to do it. Now's the time to accept the fact that your perception is either holding you back or helping you move forward.

Do you feel good when good things are happening? Most people do, but the challenge is to feel good even when good things are not happening. Why? Because bad things happen. They happen to all of us. It's inevitable. Bad things will happen to you but escaping poverty will require you to have the perspective that bad things are happening for a good reason.

I grew up in one of the worst neighborhoods in the country, where most of the men were either dead or in jail by the age of twenty-five. People were killed every day for the colors they wore; red, blue, purple and gold — none of it was worth dying for, yet people died every day. Bad things happened to me. I was molested as a child. I was verbally abused, raped and beaten, but none of those things made me feel like I was less than anyone else. None of it, and I do mean none of it, made me want to give up my dream of one day escaping poverty. In fact, it made me want to escape even more. I would even go so far as saying that it made me who I am today.

Your perception of the things that are happening in your life is either driving you forward or holding you back. My plea to you is that you find a way to use everything that's happening, both good and bad, to drive you forward. You do not have to see bad things as good things, at least not individually, but as a whole, a combination of good and bad things, may one day become the base of your strength. Having an appreciation for both may actually be a good thing. If all of this talk about you changing your perception is causing you to feel like I'm asking you to change who you are, then keep reading, so that I can help you understand why changing your perception has nothing to do with changing who you are.

Change

 The "C" word, if you ask me — and I'm no vocabulary specialist by any means — is the most feared word known to man. People are simply terrified of it. I've even heard people say, "I'm not changing for anybody!" Well, the good news is that escaping poverty won't require you to change anything about who you are. In fact, you were actually born with everything you need to make a great escape. At birth, you received every tool you need to escape one of the most difficult things in the world to escape. I guarantee you that changing your perception won't change who you are. You can still be cool. You can still be tough. You can still be strong, and you can even make mistakes. The only thing you have to do is discover more about yourself, which is not the same as changing who you are. You might have to change what you do. You might have to change where you go, but you will definitely not have to become a different person.

I remember when I made the decision to change. It happened well after my decision to escape poverty. First, I tried to escape without changing anything at all, but let me be the first to tell you, that not changing anything at all, will not work. Changes have to be made in order for you to move the first stone, so be positive about it and you'll be so much closer to freedom.

The Power of Positivity

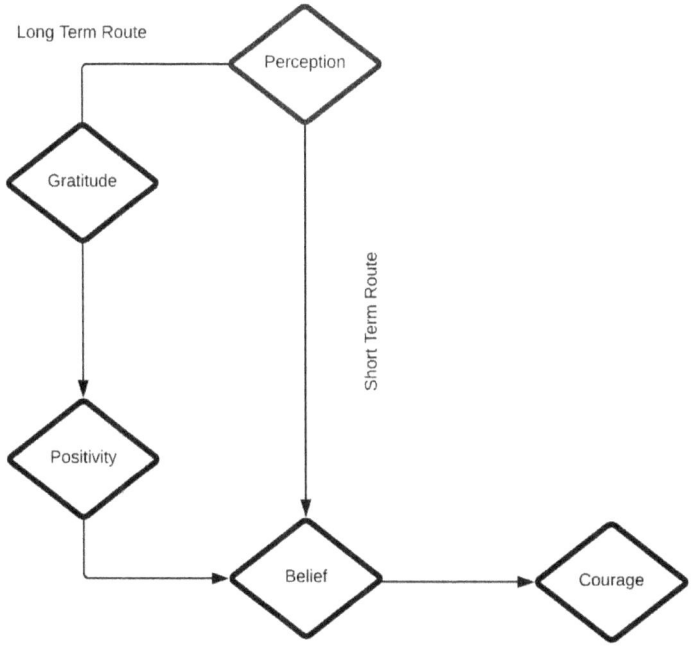

Positive energy is a powerful force that grows from a tiny seed of gratitude. The more gratitude you have, the more positive energy you have. The more positive energy you have, the stronger your belief system will be. The stronger your belief system is, the easier it is for you to be courageous. The one thing that no one escapes poverty without is courage.

There are two types of courage; long term and short term. Short term courage is used to rescue someone from a burning car or save a child from a burning house. It's no less noble than long term, but it requires only a short-term commitment. Long term courage is used for long term things like going to war overseas or being a firefighter, or police officer. If you look at the chart above, you'll see that long-term courage goes through gratitude and positivity, short term courage does not. I would encourage you to take the long-term route if you're serious about escaping poverty, because the short-term route will unfortunately lead to short term results. The path that flows through gratitude and positivity is the best one to take. It's the only one that will give you the courage you need to make your escape.

Gratitude

One of the best things I've ever learned was how to have gratitude for even the simplest things in life — a lesson I learned from Jason Forrest, owner of the Texas based company Forrest Performance Group. In one of his seminars, Jason taught my team and I the power of gratitude, and how gratitude plays a huge role in a person's ability to be courageous. Having the courage to do things you've never done before, demands a perspective that very few people have, and those who have it, understand that it all begins with gratitude.

My teenage years were full of negative energy, mostly because I was angry with my parents for abandoning me at birth. My dad left and went to the military. My mother gave me away because she didn't want to have children. In her defense, she was only a teenager, which I know, played a huge roll in her decision. She eventually took me back but by then the damage was already done. Just the knowledge of the event was enough to haunt me forever. Bouncing from house to house made me feel unwanted. I went from my mom's house to my grandmother's house, then back to my mom's house, only so I could go back to my grandmother's house again. Eventually, I ended up living with a friend, which is where I stayed until I graduated high school and left for college.

My childhood gave me a spirit of anger: one that stayed with me until I was well into my twenties. It wasn't until I learned gratitude that I was able to feel good about the bad things that happened to me. Gratitude for a combination of good and bad things, eventually gave me the drive I needed to escape poverty. Because of gratitude, those things became the evidence I needed to prove to myself, that I could escape. I even learned to have gratitude for the anger that burned inside of me. I told myself that I was so angry about the volatility of my life, that I couldn't settle for anything less than a stable one.

As you begin to change your perspective on life, don't forget about the power of gratitude. Positive energy begins with your perspective and grows from the gratitude you have for the good and bad things that happen to and for you in life. Once you change the way you look at the things that happened for you, you will realize how great you really are.

After teaching us the importance of gratitude, Jason taught us three of the most powerful words we've ever learned; I am enough. I thought about those three words every time I faced a challenge. If it wasn't for those three words, I wouldn't be where I am today, which is why I believe those three words might be of great use to you.

It's important to know that you are enough. You're enough for your friends. You're enough for your family. You're enough for your job. You're enough for your boyfriend, girlfriend, wife or husband. You're enough for that position you want to one day have. You're enough for the lifestyle you want to one day live. You're enough for your parents. You're enough for the community you live in. You have to believe you're enough to escape poverty in order to escape it. Say it right now: I am enough to escape poverty. Say it aloud. Tell yourself you can do it. Here's a list of ten powerful things that I believe you should start saying right now:

- Today, I lay the foundation for my future.
- I will stay on the path to freedom.
- I don't have to be perfect, I just have to be me.
- I am deserving of happiness.
- I am worth more than what I've been through.
- I believe in myself.
- I am a powerful, influential person.
- I am loved.
- I am wanted.
- I can and will move the first stone.

3

Believing in You

Warning

This will probably be the most controversial part of this entire book, because people who struggle with believing in themselves also struggle with believing in other people and other things. Non-believers will question every part of this chapter and find reasons to do what they've always done. Fine tuning your belief system is an important part of escaping poverty, which is why this chapter is so important. People who struggle with belief in general, need to know that they are struggling. Once they know, then they can do something about it.

Non-believers usually struggle with separating things that are true from things that are not. This could be a sticking point for you if you believe that something is true, simply because a lot of people believe it's true. There was a time when millions of people believed that the earth was flat, but we know now that those people were wrong. The earth was, and is round, no matter how many people believe otherwise. It's important to know that the truth will always be true, no matter how many people believe it's not. Once it's no longer true, then it's no longer true.

A Reliable Truth

Before we talk about how important it is to believe in yourself, let's take a moment to talk about something that lies at the foundation of each and every belief — a reliable truth. A reliable truth is a fact or belief that is trustworthy not only because it's true, but also because it has been tested and deemed trustworthy by the person or persons acting upon it.

For the sake of clarity, let's take a closer look at our definition. There are three important parts to our definition of a reliable truth. All three of them must be present for any truth to be considered reliable. First, and this should go without saying, but a reliable truth has to, at the very least, be true. It may sound like a silly thing to say, but trust me, sometimes people rely on things that are simply not true and those things we cannot and will not consider to be reliable truths. A good example of something that people rely upon that is not a reliable truth is a superstition, or a lie. Not only is a lie untrue, but it's also unreliable. So, remember, a reliable truth has to first be true.

Second, for a truth to be reliable, it has to have been tested by the person actually relying upon it; an important factor because relying upon a truth that you have not tested, is the same as taking a risk. Take a moment to think about it. It's true.

Thirdly, a reliable truth is one that has been deemed trustworthy by the person acting upon it, and is in fact, not a reliable truth to anyone who hasn't deemed it trustworthy. In other words, it doesn't matter how true it is, if you don't trust it, you're probably not going to rely upon it, thus for you, it's not a reliable truth.

You might ask yourself, "Why is all this silly stuff so important?" Well, in the absence of a reliable truth it's almost impossible to believe in even the simplest of things - including yourself. In fact, before you begin to believe in anything, you must first believe it's true and that's especially true when it comes to you believing in you. It's also true when it comes to you believing you can accomplish something or when it comes to you believing you can do something. A wise author once wrote that faith without works is dead. The same is true for a belief. A belief that has never been tested is a form of faith that demanded no work at all and is therefore unreliable. It is dead.

A reliable truth must be at the foundation of your belief in yourself, because without one, you'll find yourself like so many others. So many people in this world say they believe in themselves, but in reality, they don't. They think they do, but from what I know about believing in yourself, I can safely say they don't. I'm not talking about those who have tested their beliefs, I'm talking about those who have a genuine, but untested belief in themselves. Like for example, my friend Sharon, who always tell me that she believes in herself, but every time she sets a new goal, she comes up with three or four reasons why she can't hit it. My first question to Sharon is always the same: Why did you set a goal that you don't believe you can hit? And Sharon always responds the same way: she says, "I believe I can hit it, but..." No matter what the goal is, Sharon's response always includes some form of doubt, and that's how I know that Sharon lacks that one reliable truth that would give her the confidence she needs to truly believe in herself.

A reliable truth is important to have because you are about to do something you've never done before. My question for you is: Do you believe in yourself? If the answer is yes, then let's move on to the next question: Have you tested your belief in yourself? If not, then I would encourage you to test it as soon as possible. Some people say they believe in themselves simply because it's the popular thing to say, or perhaps they are simply too embarrassed to say they don't — I don't know. But what I do know is that people don't always tell truth when you ask them about believing in themselves. Sometimes they tell you what they think you want to hear. If that's not you, then fine. If it is, then that's fine too. All you have to do is establish a reliable truth.

It sounds like a complicated task but it's actually very simple. Let's simplify things a bit more. Imagine yourself walking towards the edge of a cliff. Your eyes are covered with a blindfold. Your friend is holding you by the arm. The wind is high. You feel the wind blowing against your face. In your ear, there's a familiar voice. It's the voice of your friend and he or she is telling you, "Relax everything's going to be okay." This is hard to believe because just beneath your toes the ground has come to an end. You're definitely standing at the edge of a cliff. Not only have you never stood at the edge of this cliff before, but you have never seen what's at the bottom of it. A situation like this demands a reliable truth because without one you're probably not going to jump. If you've never stood at the edge of this very cliff, then you're probably not going to believe your friend when he or she says, "The cliff is only 4 feet high and there's a huge pile of hay at the bottom to break your fall." Some of us though, would trust our friends and jump. Why? Because their words have in the past proven to be reliable.

Although jumping may not be the wisest thing to do, a decision to do so based on a truth that has been tested is at the very least, understandable. Take a look at the following example. Hopefully it will help you understand a little bit more about reliable truths.

Example

Last month, Amy won Employee of the Year for the second year in a row. At the company meeting, her supervisor recognized her for going above and beyond her required duties. As he handed her the award, he smiled because he knew she would be just as humble as she was the year before. Her coworkers cheered her on as she stood at the podium in her own uncomfortable way. They knew exactly what she was going to say because she was still the same, predictable Amy. After she thanked her coworkers, lowered her head and returned to her seat, her supervisor continued to recognize her for things that she thought went unnoticed.

The next day, her supervisor approached her about a new position in the company. He explained how the position would be a step up, and why he felt like she would be the perfect fit. The position came with a little more responsibility, so Amy turned it down, just as she did when he offered her the last two positions. Even though she'd won Employee of the Year two years in a row, Amy was still afraid that she would fail.

So many people are just like Amy; they can't see the reliable truth that's right in front of their faces. They pass on once-in-a-lifetime opportunities, simply because they don't know how great they truly are. But those who understand the value of a reliable truth, understand how important it is to build on past accomplishments. The road to believing in yourself begins with a reliable truth.

Believing in You

You have finally made it to what I consider to be the single most important section in this entire book. The importance of believing in yourself cannot be overstated. Can you win without believing in yourself? Yes. Can you be successful without believing in yourself? No, because eventually, somewhere on the path to success, you'll fail and when you do, your belief in yourself will be the only thing you can count on.

Your belief in someone else won't help you. Neither will your belief in luck, nor your belief in a process, system or religion; and I'm not saying that God can't or won't continue to bless you, what I'm saying is that your blessings will be hard to keep if you don't believe you can do what it takes to keep them.

Success is not about luck or how many times you can get lucky. It's about making the right decisions at the right time and doing what it takes to make the outcomes of those decisions work for you. The time to believe in yourself is now, and to do so, you need to establish a reliable truth; one that has to do with you and no one else.

Believing in someone else will not help you succeed. It might inspire you, but it will not make you successful. You need to rely on your own abilities to remain successful over a prolonged period of time. Your success begins and ends with you believing in you. Think long and hard, right now, about what you've accomplished in life. No matter how small of a victory it was, it might be the one thing that propels you forward in the future. What is your reliable truth? Think about it; it's important that you have one.

After the Music

I remember when I first began to believe in myself. I was in Jackson, Mississippi auditioning for a music contract with DeVante from the R&B group Jodeci. Like most of the young men in Jacktown, I saw music as my only way out of poverty, so this event was an opportunity that I couldn't pass up. The nightclub was packed with onlookers and all of them were anxious to see who the winner would be. Artist after artist took to the stage to wow the crowd with their lyrical prowess. Some of the best performers in the area showed up for a chance to take advantage of the only big music-related opportunity of the summer. I waited patiently for my turn, but it was in no way an easy wait. I was nervous. I was just as nervous as you would've been. As a young kid growing up in poverty, landing a music contract was the easiest way out and I was the closest I'd ever been to making it happen.

When I took the stage, I saw a few eyes in the crowd light up. It gave me the confidence I needed to get off to a good start. Somehow, on that night, I finished amongst the finalist. The crowd enjoyed every minute of my performance, which was surprising, because I performed a song that I'd written only a few days before. Not only that, but my producer and I spent a lot of time coming up with the beat, but very little time at all practicing the song over the beat. In the end though, it was a success. My producer was probably just as surprised as I was because we were both amateurs compared to the other performers on stage that night.

I'm sharing this story with you because it was the first time that I truly believed I could be great. It was an achievement that later became my reliable truth, and the one true reminder that I could do anything that I put my mind to. Yes, it was only a small step towards greatness, but at least it was a step in the right direction.

I came from nothing, to where I am today. I believe you can do the same if you learn how to establish a reliable truth; a truth that you can look back on every time you face a challenge. Once you've established your own reliable truth, you'll be able to approach every challenge with the mindset that you've won before, so why not now.

Opportunities

Opportunities are like walking into the darkness. At first, you don't see a thing, but then your eyes adjust, and things begin to take form. What I'm trying to say is be patient, believe in yourself and trust your instincts. Opportunities don't come every day, but one day, you'll get one, and when you do, you need to take full advantage of it.

I learned years ago that opportunities are not easy to recognize, so the best advice I can give you is to keep your eyes open, be ready, know yourself and know your abilities. Believe you can do things that you've never done before. Be watchful. Keeping your eyes open for even the smallest of opportunities will dramatically increase your chances of escaping poverty.

Success waits for no one, so be ready. You may not feel like you're ready, but believe me, you are. All you have to do is believe. Be courageous. If you change your perspective of the things that are happening to you, you can make them work for you.

Believe in yourself and have the courage to believe that you can escape poverty just as others have before you. It all begins within you. By changing the way you look at things, you can move the first set of stones on the path to your escape. The optics are no match for you now that you know how to move them.

Be Inspired

If you're waiting for someone else to inspire you, then you're waiting for something that may never happen. Not many people are inspiring enough to inspire someone to escape poverty. Your inspiration to escape should begin with you. It should begin with the light that shines within you, or in other words, it should begin within your optics.

You should wake up in the morning and inspire yourself. Yes, you should inspire yourself, long before anyone else even gets a chance to. Regardless of what others are doing, you should be doing the best you can do, every chance you get to do it. That type of drive demands inspiration.

I can honestly say that I don't know any successful people who can say that they've never been inspired. Inspiration plays a significant role in every successful person's life. It appears on the path to success in many forms, and it will be on the path to your escape just the same.

4

Understanding the Pressures

Enough is Enough

The moment that changed everything for me, happened while I was in my early twenties. Yet I still remember it like it was just yesterday. On that cold summer night, rain fell through the trees like the leaves weren't even there. My clothes were soaked, my face was wet, the ground was muddy, and I had every reason to believe that things were going to get even worse.

No matter which way I turned, the wind blew rain into my eyes and face, so I had no choice but to come up with another place to sleep. I rushed over to the men's dormitory at Jackson State University, where I braced myself for a long and uncomfortable night.

I sat down in the stairway with my elbows spread out and my back against the steps. My head was tired, wet and heavy. All I could do was lean back and let it rest in between my shoulders. My lashes were soaked, chill bumps covered my arms, but worst of all, my butt was as numb as could be.

My break through moment came at about three in the morning, when a young man came up the stairs and stepped next to me, leaving a puddle of mud that just happened to be in the same spot that I was resting my elbow. When he passed by, I placed my arm right in the spot he left behind, and I sat there for a minute, with a strange feeling of comfort in my mind and not even a care in my spirit.

In that moment, I felt my optics shift. The light that shined within me slowly turned towards my perception of myself. It revealed something that I'd never seen before. It was there and I could see it. For the first time, I could see my path to freedom, and it looked exactly like the map on the following page. That's when I knew that I had to get through the Pressures in order to create the Behaviors that I needed to survive the Pitfalls. So yes, I was homeless, but I was humble. I was patient and I was ready.

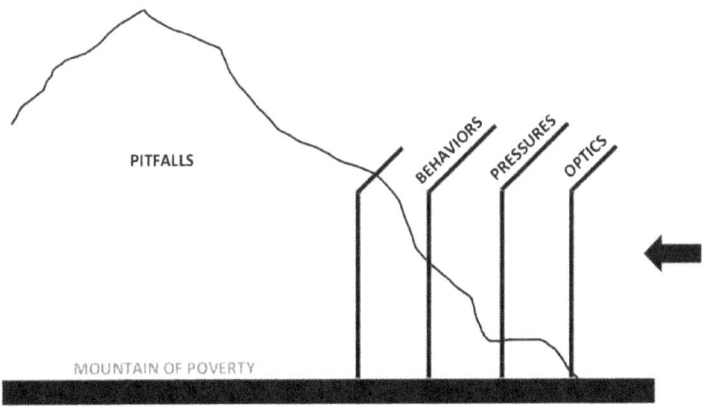

Embracing Failure

Every time I thought about escaping poverty, I thought about failure; the greatest pressure of all. Much like change, failure is one of the most feared words in the human vocabulary. It's the fear of failure that stands in between capable people and the opportunities that are available to them. Opportunities are all around you, but they may not look or sound like you want them to. They may sound and look challenging, but you can't be afraid of a challenge. You can't be afraid to try something you've never done before. You have to be willing to try it and fail.

Successful people fail all the time. The only difference between them and everyone else is that they bounce back like nothing ever happened. It's important to know that you will eventually fail but when you do, you must embrace it. You must be willing to learn from each and every one of your failures.

Failure is not what most people think it is. If you look at it as an opportunity to learn, you can increase your opportunity to escape poverty. In fact, you can even increase your chances of being successful. That's the goal. Escaping poverty will require you to fail and bounce back like nothing ever happened. You will not be successful at everything you try, but it's important to maintain your composure and understand that failure is inevitable.

You and Others

The fear of failure spawns from a disbelief in your abilities and is in fact, closely linked to the idea that failure will result in you disappointing yourself and others. What I want you to know is that the fear of failure and the disappointment you feel when others see you fail, ultimately become the gravitational force that holds the second stone firmly in place. To move the second stone, you not only have to believe in yourself, but you also have to be okay with other people seeing you fail. Of course, no one wants to fail, but as I said earlier, failure is inevitable. Surrounding yourself with people who can encourage you, even when you fail, is not a bad idea. That's why this next section is so important.

Friends, Family and People

It's never a good idea to make blanket statements, but I'm going to make this one, even though it's not true one hundred percent of the time. So, here's my not really true, but true enough statement: the people that are the closest to you, your friends and your family, will be the last ones to believe in you. I've talked to enough of my own friends to know that friends and family don't believe in you until they have real evidence of your success. Sometimes they wait until other people deem you successful, then they hop on board like they've been with you the entire time. Sometimes they wait to see how many new and expensive things you buy before they give you their support. It's disappointing, but you have to get through it. The worst thing you can do is wait for other people to believe in you. You absolutely cannot wait for people who have no stake in your escape. You simply cannot and I repeat, cannot let people dictate how you feel about yourself. You can't become emotional when people doubt your abilities, and you definitely can't give up every time one of your friends, or family members think you should be doing something different.

Relationships

I like to look at relationships from an investment point of view. They are either good, bad, useful or useless. Every year, I categorize each of my investments as either good and useful, good but useless, bad but useful, or bad and useless. I do the same thing for my relationships, because it allows me to give them value and purpose.

Good Relationships

Good relationships are always good to have. I like to think of them as good investments. Like good investments, every time you put something in, you get something out, which is obviously the goal. If I break even on a good investment, then I consider that investment to be good but useless. Relationships are no different. If I get back exactly what I put into a good relationship, then I see that relationship as good but useless. I'm not saying it's a bad relationship, but if it's not adding value to my life, then it's certainly not good and useful. The only time I categorize a relationship as good and useful is when I get back more than what I put into it. I hope that makes sense. Now let's take a look at bad relationships.

Bad Relationships

Whenever I break even in a bad relationship, I consider that relationship to be bad but useful. When I take a loss in a bad relationship, I categorize that relationship to be bad and useless. Keep in mind that useless relationships are not always bad, but like bad relationships they are bad investments. Every time you put something in, you get absolutely nothing in return. In fact, you end up with a quantifiable negative, which is the worst-case scenario.

Activity

Take a look at the diagram on the next page and think about the people you have in your life. If you have a good relationship with someone and you get back more than what you put into the relationship, then put that person's name in the good and useful box. If you get back exactly what you put in, then go ahead and put that person's name in the good but useless box. It's important to remember that the person is not useless, only the relationship.

Now, let's move down to the bad category. If you have a bad relationship with someone and you get back exactly what you put into the relationship, then write that person's name in the bad but useful box. If you get back less, then write that person's name in the bad and useless box. By the time you're done, you should have at least one name in every box. Continue.

	USEFUL	USELESS
GOOD		
BAD		

Example 1

Monica has a significant other that lives with her in her two-bedroom apartment. He has no job, no goals and no way to help her pay the bills. He has nothing. He can't keep a job, because for some reason he thinks he can walk into a company and tell them what he is, and isn't, going to do. Every time Monica asks him about getting a job, he gets an attitude.

Meanwhile, he eats up all of the food that Monica buys for her children. He has children outside of the relationship, but he does nothing to support them. It's clear that Monica loves him more than anything in the world. In fact, she can't live without him, but regardless, she put his name in the bad and useless box. Monica already knows that he is not good for her, even though she can't seem to let him go.

Example 2

An example of a good but useless relationship for Monica is the relationship she has with her mother. She loves her mother and her mother loves her. But every time Monica talks about doing something to improve her life, her mother gives her every reason why she shouldn't do it. Since Monica is always positive and her mother is always negative, the two of them are never on the same page. When Monica needs her mother's support, her mother can't be found, mainly because she spends every other night in the bar drinking and dancing. Her mother allows her to live with her, but the two of them split the bills and share the groceries. For those reasons Monica put her mother Martha's name in the good and useful box, even though she really should've put it in the good and useless box. Just because you have a good relationship with someone you love, doesn't mean that the person adds value to your life. If you can't get a physical, emotional or financial gain from a relationship, then how much is the relationship really helping you?

Example 3

Monica has a good and useful relationship with her co-worker Sharon, who sends her inspirational quotes twice a week. She tells her how much she believes in her and encourages her to try new things. When Monica is feeling down, Sharon goes out of her way to lift her up. In return, Monica helps Sharon with her kids. When Sharon drops them off at practice, Monica picks them up. When Sharon has to work late, Monica takes them home with her. Since

Sharon is invaluable in Monica's life, she put Sharon's name in the good and useful box.

Example 4

Tracy keeps the kids at night while Monica goes to school. Even though they argue every week, Tracy still opens the door for Monica and the kids. Monica knows for sure that Tracy is the only person that's willing to keep her terrible kids, so she truly appreciates Tracy for the sacrifices she makes. Her mother refuses to keep her kids, so without Tracy, Monica would be screwed. For that reason, Monica put Tracy's name in the bad but useful box.

The Purpose

This activity is designed to help you identify the people who add no value to your life. The goal is to either get more out of them or move them out of your life altogether. For those who add value to your life, you should invest more time and energy. Those are the people who will help you escape. For everyone else, set clear expectations and be ready to let them go if they can't meet them.

Things

It's hard to keep up with the Joneses when you don't have the type of money that the Joneses have. Clothes, cars, homes, diamonds and all the toys money can buy — that's what people think of when they think of success, but you can be successful without any of it. Success is not about what you have, it's about how many people you help with what you have.

The ownership of material things always has and always will be a sign of success for people who have money and people who don't, but if you don't have the money, you shouldn't be buying things that people with money buy. I like Jordans as much as everyone else, but I've never owned a pair. I've seen so many people trying to escape poverty while trying to buy things that people with money have. It never works. That's why I'm telling you now that it won't work. Basketball players don't pay your bills. Football players don't pay your bills. Actors and actresses don't pay your bills and neither do clothing manufacturers, so wasting your money on things they make or promote is a bad idea.

The pressure is real when it comes to material things. We all want them, even when we know we can't afford them. Can we buy them? Yes, but not without experiencing a major setback. We all have bills and expenses, both of which have to be paid, but sometimes we want what we want and when we do, we buy things that cause us to fall further behind on the things that we should be using our money on. If you want to escape poverty, then you need to know when and when not to buy things. Name brand clothes can wait. Gold chains and expensive shoes can wait. Overpriced purses can wait. Drugs, cigarettes and alcohol can wait. Cover charges at the nightclub can wait too. Trust me, they can.

Artificial Power

Some people actually decrease their chances of escaping poverty by chasing what I call artificial power. We all know people who walk, talk and act like they can make things happen but every time they try to make something happen, they can't. A lot of these people have nice things but no money in the bank. Many of them have a flawed understanding of respect and consequently, receive no respect from people who actually have real power. They may own a few nice things, but that's about it. They may even look like they have money all the time but just beneath the surface they are as broke as you are.

Millions of people have died chasing what they believed to be money, power and respect, but many of them actually died chasing money, a skewed version of respect and yes, artificial power. In the inner city, people die every day for nothing more than the respect of the people around them. They make mistakes they can't afford to make. They do things they can't afford to do, and they waste time that they can't afford to waste.

The pursuit of artificial power will distract from your goal of escaping poverty. You can't afford to waste time, money and energy trying to obtain something that will do nothing for you long term. Real power shows itself in those who understand that respect is more about getting others to believe in you, than it is about making yourself look like a boss. The ability to influence those around you in a positive way is what true power is all about, and anything short of that is artificial.

The Hustle

My cousin hustles her butt off every day. She makes five dollars here and five dollars there, but by the end of the day she has nothing to show for it. She wants to live a good life just like everyone else, but she can't because the everyday hustle has her going in circles. Her hustle is the worst kind of hustle you can have. You know, the kind that pays just enough for you to live the kind of lifestyle that you already hate to live. Right now, she's living what she calls the struggle. She's living the hard life; the kind of life that makes you look old before you've really had a chance to even live.

I lived in the struggle long enough to know that the struggle is real. I remember those days when I worked hard all day for long hours just so I could finish off the week with nothing. I started my hustle as a kid babysitting for my aunt Debra and my cousin Shawn. I made a few dollars a night, but I used it all to buy cookies and candy. Then I started making sketches and selling them for a dollar each. While the people around me were selling drugs, I was getting my money the legal way, because I knew that I couldn't possibly sell enough drugs to get out of the ghetto.

I tell people all the time that drug money is not the way out of poverty. So, if you're selling drugs, you need to stop it. If you're breaking in houses and selling the goods you stole, you need to stop that too.

If your hustle doesn't pay at least fifty grand a year, then you need a new hustle. Time is just too precious for you to be spending it chasing peanuts. A real hustle has the potential to get you out of the situation that you're in, so take a look at your hustle and see if it pays the bills. If it doesn't, then add in an additional hustle, or get rid of your hustle all together.

Inspiration

If you weren't inspired to read this book, you probably wouldn't be reading it. Not only that but if you weren't inspired to escape poverty, you probably wouldn't be trying to escape it. If you weren't inspired to follow the map, you probably wouldn't be following it, so I can't stress enough the importance of inspiration. On the path to your escape, inspiration begins within your optics, but occurs within every phase of your escape. You won't take full advantage of opportunities unless you're inspired to. You won't change your behavior unless you're inspired to. You have to have a reason to change and that reason may very well be inspiration.

When you fail, you need to pick up and try again, which may be hard to do if you're not inspired to do so. It's important to know that uninspired people usually settle for what they have, instead of pushing forward until they have what they want. You cannot be one of those people. You cannot be uninspired and escape poverty, so I suggest that you either learn how to inspire yourself or find people who can inspire you. If your friends, family, associates, or coworkers can't inspire you, then you need to put yourself around people who can.

5
Understanding the Behaviors

The Road to Discovery

So now that you've moved the first two stones, the Optics and the Pressures, it's time to talk about the third and most difficult stone to move; the Behaviors. Once you've changed your perception, learned gratitude, stacked up on positive energy, learned to believe in yourself and developed enough courage to take on the Pressures; then and only then will you be ready to take the next step and establish the behaviors that will help you get through the Pitfalls. Sustainable success is the sum of good behaviors, which is why it's so important for you to know what those behaviors are and where to find them if you don't.

See Greatness

It's a known fact that people who live in poverty behave differently than people who live in more prominent areas — and that's not to say that rich people do everything right, but to simply say that rich people and poor people tend to do things differently. Before we dive into the importance of changing your behavior, I want to point out one important fact, because sometimes we take for granted the fact that people with money actually had to do something to get it. I want to acknowledge right now, the fact that people with money had to do something to get and to keep the money that they have. I think it's important that we open our eyes and see the behaviors that make great people great and recognize them for doing the things that made them great, because that's the only way that we'll ever be able to give the correct amount of importance to the things that they did to be as great as they are.

The behaviors that make great people great are not always easy to identify. Sometimes you have to look for them and even then, you might not find what you're looking for. So, for the sake of time, I'm simply going to tell you what makes great people great, instead of letting you stumble your way down the road to discovery.

Just Do It

To escape poverty, you have to be willing to change the way you do things, as well as the way you handle things, especially those things that are important to your escape, like for example, money, bills, expenses, and relationships. You have to change how you handle all of those things to actually improve your circumstances. To better yourself, you have to do some things that you've never done before, or perhaps do some things that you've done before, but in a different way.

On the path to freedom, you have to learn some things that you've never learned before, or maybe even trust some people that you've never trusted before, but whatever the case, escaping poverty will require you to step out on faith and do something different. I'm asking that you trust me, right now and refer to the map that I gave you, because, like I said earlier, knowing where you are in the process is important.

The Big Three

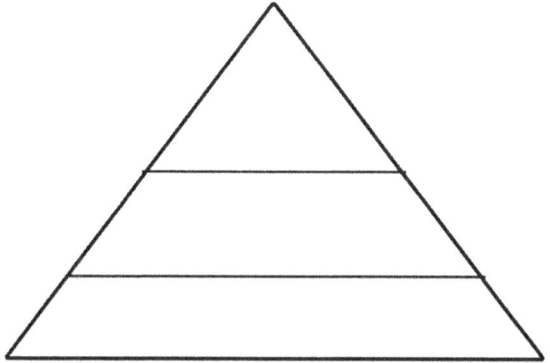

Before writing this book, I asked a hundred people this question: What one thing did you do that made you successful? Almost all of them said something different, but as I made a list of what they said, I realized that many of them were saying the same thing but in a different way. There were three things that appeared on the list more often than any others and those three things I would like to share with you today.

1 Work Hard

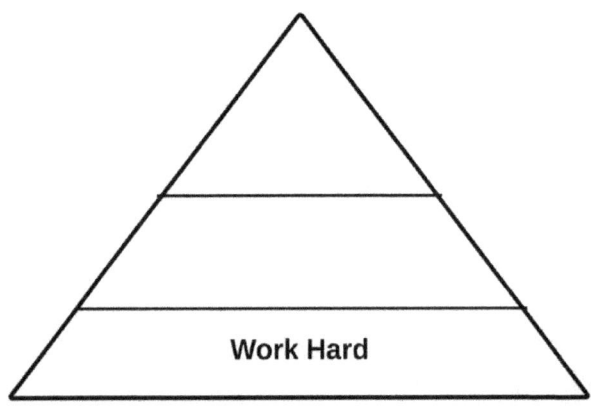

Working at Cintas, the uniform company, gave me the opportunity to develop the work ethic that I have today. My supervisor Harry Miggins was a hardworking man. He worked every day like he cared more about doing a good job than anything thing else. Even when the conditions weren't favorable, he showed up on time and worked until the job was done. Sometimes it was hot, sometimes it was freezing cold, but nothing stopped him from doing satisfactory work.

Our customers demanded quality work and timely deliveries, which is why Harry taught my team and I to be diligent in our work. We worked long hours for very little money, but that didn't stop us from working hard and having fun. Unlike some supervisors, Harry believed that fun was the secret to getting employees to come to work. He always said, "It's easier to do a good job when you love what you do and have fun doing it." So, for us, every day was a good day, even the bad ones.

When I left Cintas, I took Harry's approach to work and made it my own. I knew that I had to work hard if I wanted to be noticed by upper management. The only way to become a supervisor like Harry, was to work as hard as Harry worked. I can't put it any simpler than that. Hard work gets rewarded, so to escape poverty, I knew that I had to work hard and put myself in position to be noticed.

The best way to get a new opportunity is to work hard on the one that you have. Hard work plays an important role in you getting more opportunities, which ultimately will help you make your escape. The best way to avoid failure is to work hard. The best way to move the first three stones is to work hard, it's as simple as that. Working hard really did make a difference for all of the people that interviewed for this book, but they had more to say, so let's continue on with our list.

2 Listen

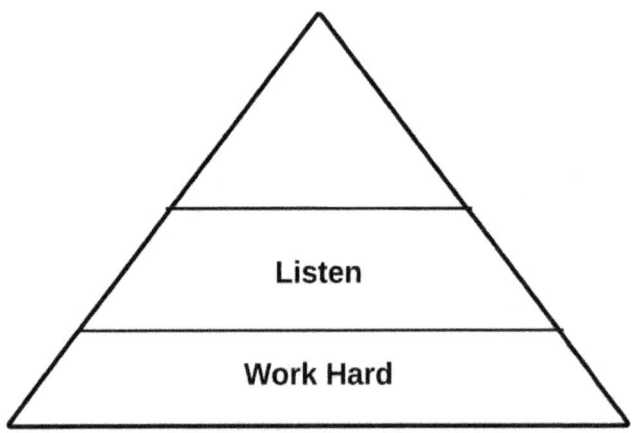

Listening is not just an important part of communication, it plays an important role in your escape. If your ears are not open to opportunities, then you will definitely miss them. You have to be paying attention to what's happening around you to recognize opportunities for what they are. You can't afford to be closed minded when opportunities come your way. You need to be mindful of the fact that opportunities come in many forms, some of which you've never thought of before.

New opportunities often require you to listen to someone who has done them before. The fastest way to blow a new opportunity is to not listen to the person that's giving it to you. Experience is the best teacher for sure, but you can learn a lot from someone with more experience than you have.

Several times over the course of my career, I've offered new opportunities to people, and I can tell you from experience that the people who blew them were the people who didn't listen. When I told them to apply for the job today, they applied two days later. When I told them to reach out to a certain person, they reached out to someone else instead. When I told them to research the company before going in for an interview, they went in for the interview with no knowledge of the company. No matter what I said, they did the opposite.

Successful people understand that listening is a skill that very few people have, which is why so many of the one hundred people that I spoke with, wanted me to stress to you the importance of listening. You see, successful people understand that most things can be taught, but it's hard to teach anything to someone who won't listen.

I would rather hire someone with no experience at all, than to hire someone who won't listen. Like I said, the fastest way to blow an opportunity is to not listen, so listen to those who have escaped poverty before and increase your chances of one day making your own escape.

The last thing on our list was the most reoccurring response given by the one hundred people who interviewed. It was kind of a no brainer, but it was given by each person with passion, commitment and a lot of thought, which is why I simply couldn't leave it out of this book. After so many people said it, I started to understand its importance because maybe, just maybe, there are some people out there that don't know how important it really is. What is it? Well, to sum it up, it's the ability to overcome.

3 Overcome

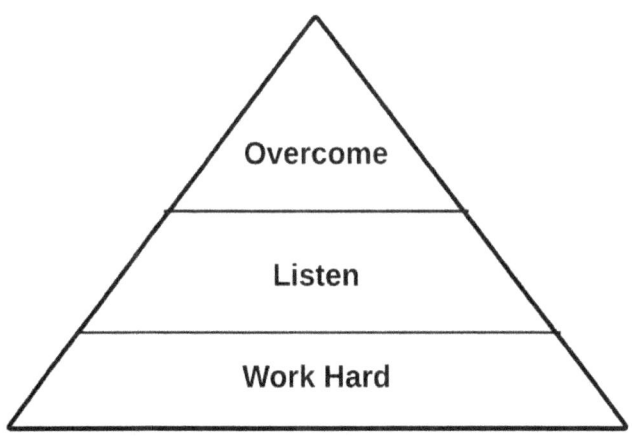

Maybe you've heard it referred to as perseverance, determination, will, grit or tenacity, but it all boils down to the same thing and that's the ability to overcome challenging situations. All of the one hundred people interviewed for this book overcame something to get to where they are. None of them escaped poverty without first overcoming their fears or slaying their demons so to speak. Each and every one of them experienced trials and tribulations along the way, but they fought through them; They didn't give up and didn't quit. To escape poverty, you have to overcome not just your fears, but you have to overcome your shortcomings and all of the other things that might be holding you back. Depression, anxiety, low self-esteem, arrogance, stubbornness — it can all get in the way. Drug abuse, alcoholism, molestation, neglect, verbal abuse, rape — all of it can be overcome.

A friend told me once that everything you go through makes you stronger than you were before you had to go through it. I not only believe what he said, but I've lived it and experienced it, so I can say with firsthand knowledge, that it's true. Overcoming your problems will definitely make you stronger, but to maintain your strength you have to do something that only one of the one hundred people interviewed for this book had the wisdom to say; you have to make the right choices and avoid the pitfalls.

Honorable Mention

I get it. They say home is where the heart is, but sometimes you and your heart need to pick up and move. While talking with retired chemist, Juan Sanders, I heard something that I believe is so important that I just can't leave it out of this book. Juan is a graduate from Hampton University, that grew up in poverty just like you and I, but somehow, he broke free of his chains and became the man that he is today.

According to Juan, the one thing that made the biggest difference in his life, was the opportunity to see something different. By visiting other cities, he gained a new perspective on life. Different people, different roads, different kinds of trees, different types of weather, and all of the experiences that came with those things, challenged Juan to open up and be more vocal. The freshness of it all inspired him to let himself out of the box. It didn't just show him a different way to live, it encouraged him to live a different way.

It's hard to know what's out there if you haven't gone out there. Your little circle will only show you a small portion of what's available to you. There is so much more that the world has for you, but you have to go out and get it. Face it, sometimes what you need is not at home; It's somewhere else.

6

Surviving the Pitfalls

The One

The one category that towers above all others is the same one that promises to break you down to the lowest point in your life, but that's if, and only if, you're not careful. Once you've changed your optics, survived the pressures and learned the right behaviors, you can then take your first step into the Pitfalls, but keep in mind though that the Pitfalls are as deep as life itself.

The one mistake that should never be made is the one that sends you tumbling back to poverty, and that mistake always happens in the Pitfalls. To avoid making that one crucial mistake, all you have to do is make the right choices. One of the one hundred people interviewed for this book walked me through some of the choices that he made in his life. He explained to me how each of them made a difference in his life and where he would be if he hadn't made those decisions the way that he did. When the conversation was done, I understood completely how each of those decisions could've taken his life down a different path.

Decisions and Consequences

For every decision you make, there's a consequence that may or may not work out in your favor. My friend Mike would tell you the same thing if he was alive, but unfortunately, he made a decision that cost him his life. My use-to-be best friend Tim would tell you the exact same thing as well, because one day he made a decision that caused him to spend half of his life in prison and he regrets it.

Tim and I hung together every day in high school, but we made different decisions in life and those decisions made all the difference. I remember when he was breaking in houses and getting into fights. I was focused on my homework and trying to pass my classes, while he was trying to come up as a gang member and street thug. I have to believe that my life is better today because of my decision to stay away from bad things. It's been twenty-three years since high school, and we are still making our decisions in different ways. My decisions are all made through a slow and thoughtful process and his decisions are all made in a hurry. The best thing you can do for yourself is to give a lot of thought to each and every one of your decisions, that way you can avoid the mistakes that so many others have made. Take your time and make each decision like they matter, because they do.

The Dollar Effect

I would be doing you a disservice if I didn't spend some time talking about the bad things that happen in your life every time things seem to be going in the right direction. They have a lot to do with the decisions you make so this is the perfect time to talk about them. As you already know, you cannot escape poverty by making bad decisions.

The little things always come back to haunt you, which is something I saw in my own life. Every time I thought I was doing good something bad would happen. As soon as I got a few dollars in my pocket my car would break down, my furnace would go out, or something crazy would happen that would cause me to spend even more money than I initially thought. I call it the Dollar Effect, because every time you earn a new dollar, the other things going on in your life create an unexpected demand for that dollar; one that causes an unavoidable burden on your finances.

I know the Dollar Effect is real, because I've met hundreds of people going through the same thing that I went through. Every time they make a few bucks, they end up spending it all on an unexpected catastrophe. Not that I believe in getting tax refunds, but every time my friends got tax money, they had to spend it all on bills. Every time my family members won money at the casino, they ended up spending it on car repairs or late fees.

The Dollar Effect is a real phenomenon that hunts people in poverty. You have to escape it and the only way to do so is to make smart decisions. Every money related decision you make has to be made with the Dollar Effect in mind. To escape poverty, you have to avoid buying things that will cost you money down the road. You can't afford to buy things that only provide you with short term satisfaction, or things that break down before you can get your money's worth.

Take a look at the clothes you buy. Are you buying a brand or are you buying a quality product that will serve you long term? If you're not buying clothes that you can wear for at least the next 5 to 10 years, then you're making a big mistake. If you're not buying cars that won't break down in the next ten years, then you're buying the wrong kind of cars. When you're escaping poverty, you don't have the funds to replace things you've already bought. In short, you should be buying quality products at the lowest possible prices.

Wants and Needs

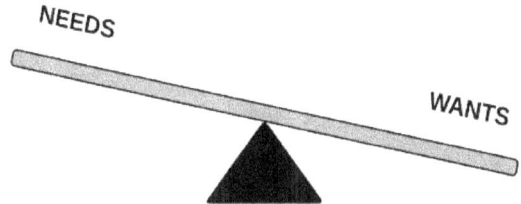

Do you need what you want, or do you want what you need? That's the question I asked myself right before I decided to eliminate the Dollar Effect from my life. A new outfit every weekend had me looking great at the club, but as soon as the next bill came in the mail, I instantly became a sight for sore eyes. My pockets were hurt, my bank account was empty, and my pride was lower than the fuel gauge in my car. I knew I had to pay for those outfits for a long time, because once I got behind on my bills, there was no chance of me catching up.

I made that mistake over and over again for a couple years, but then, finally, I realized that my wants came second to my needs. Did I need a new outfit? No. Did I want a new outfit? Yes, but not as much as I wanted and needed financial stability. When your temporary wants outweigh your long term wants and needs, financial stability, for you, becomes impossible. The decision to give more weight to my needs, ultimately led to my financial freedom.

How Bad Do You Want It?

We've all heard at least one or two people claim to be self-made millionaires, but of course they can't be self-made if somebody had to buy what they were selling. No matter what they tell you, the truth is that no one makes it through the pitfalls without at least a little bit of help. The fastest way to get through is to ask for help, so you can't be afraid to ask people who've done it before to show you how they did.

I understand that sometimes it's hard to come up with the right questions, or perhaps humble yourself enough to tell someone that they're doing better than you are, but hopefully there will come a point in your life where your success will be more important than your ego. There's no reason to be ashamed about wanting to grow or wanting to create a better life so that you can do more for the people around you.

I understand that you might not know the right people to talk to — I've been there before. I didn't have any successful people in my network and that made it more difficult for me to find the answers that I needed. It takes courage to reach out to people that you don't know and ask them personal questions about their lives, but once you do it, you'll see that successful people love to tell others how they became successful. In fact, many of them have been looking for people just like you; people that they can share their stories with and make a difference in their lives.

I didn't believe that was true before I began to reach out to them with questions, but once I found the courage to open my mouth and ask, I found them to be very open and honest with me. All of them gave me solid advice that I could use. If you're struggling with finding the right questions, here's a list that I think you will find most useful:

- How hard was it for you to find success?
- How did you get your first real opportunity?
- Who or what inspired you along the way?
- What advice helped you the most?
- When did you believe you could be successful?
- How many times have you failed at something?
- What advice would you give me?
- What changes did you make in life?
- How long did it take you to get where you are?
- How did you manage your time along the way?

If you want it bad enough, then you'll find someone to ask the ten questions on the list above. Your escape from poverty may very well depend on the information that you get from the people you put yourself around. Don't wait for them to find you. Seek them out and get the advice that you need. Some things should not be learned the hard way.

The Advantage

If you've looked for a job in the last ten years, then you know that it takes forever to find a job. The application process is longer than it's ever been. Almost every company has an online test, and that's in addition to the online application. Even if you score the best score on the test, you still have to go through the interview process, which can include three, and sometimes four interviews. You're doing good if you make it to the second interview, because some people spend eight hours a day for months filling out applications and only get one interview. I've done it, so I know all too well how frustrating it can be to find a job. If I could give you one, valuable piece of information, it would be this: The best way to shorten your job search is to learn how to prepare for an interview.

There are some great websites online that talk extensively about how to prepare for an interview, but I'm going to sum it all up so that you can be one step ahead of everyone else. It all comes down to one word, and that one word is value. When you go to an interview without a clear understanding of your value, you are essentially, walking into the biggest moment of your life without the one thing that you need to succeed. People who know their value have an advantage over those who don't.

One really good way to identify your true value as an employee, is to go back and print out the job descriptions for all of your previous jobs. On those job descriptions you'll find a list of duties, responsibilities, skills and many other valuable things that companies at some point, hired you for. All of those things count towards your value, but no one will know what they are, unless you tell them. You need to know exactly what they are for that reason because employers depend on you to tell them what you're worth.

The worst thing you can do is go into an interview and undervalue yourself. I've interviewed hundreds of people over the course of my career and I can tell you, that those who undervalued themselves didn't get the job. No matter how many jobs you've had, you still have some type of value. Even people who haven't had a job, have value. High school students, for example, have value. College students have value. Gang members, drug dealers and even people in prison have value. They all bring things to the table that employers need, and so do you. You should know that you are special and unique. You have skills and a perspective that no one else has. Your thoughts and ideas are worth something. In fact, the next big idea may very well be within you. The only way to get the job that you really want is to learn how to sell your value, regardless of how many jobs you've had, or what you've done. Business is all about sales and it always will be. If you can sell yourself, then you can be the next big thing in business.

No one should know more about you than you, because you've been with you since the day you were born. After all that time, you should have an advantage over anyone else when it comes to you. You should know what you bring to the table, and you should know your abilities. Employers shouldn't have to pull that information out of you during an interview. It should all come out naturally. So right now, I would encourage you to write down five good things about yourself that you offer any employer. Here's a list of examples:

- I've always had great vision. I can lead people.
- I'm great with customers. I can help you grow.
- I'm creative. I bring a lot of new ideas to the table.
- I'm very detailed. I can help improve processes.
- I'm passionate about my work. I'm productive.

Before you go to your next interview, practice saying at least five good things about yourself. Make sure that all five things have some type of value to the company you're interviewing with. Once you can say those five things with confidence, you can go into any interview feeling like you deserve to be hired.

Employment

Since you can't work your way out of poverty without a job, getting a job should be at the top of your list of things to do. But before you rush out and get two or three jobs, you should think about how that decision affects everything else in your life. Making the right employment decisions can shorten the amount of time it takes for you to escape, but the wrong decisions could have you in poverty for the rest of your life. If you want to escape poverty and maintain a consistent lifestyle, then there's some things you need to know about employment.

Some people work more hours than they should, just to make a decent living. They trade money for precious moments with friends and family, but that's no way to go about living. You need to balance out your time on the job with the time you spend with your loved ones. You can't mentally burn out and stay the course. I know people who work two or three jobs, just because they can't find a job that pays a good salary. Working long hours is not good for you or your family. I don't think you should do it. I think you should keep looking, until you find one job that pays the bills, all on its own.

If you have two jobs that you love doing, then keep them, but I don't recommend you keeping any job that don't pay you what you're worth. Here's my definition of a good job: A good job is any legal activity that pays you what you're worth. I might even expand on that definition and say that a good job pays you what you believe you're worth. I hate defining it that way, but I do, because I know a lot of talented people who always seem to settle for less than what they're worth.

When you're trying to escape poverty, you can't settle for the first job you can get. You have to find a way to get the job that you truly need. You need a job that can help you escape. The effort you put into getting the right job will make all the difference in the world. Remember your value and don't take anything less than that. Use the things you've done in the past to help you get that one job that will help you make your escape. Focus on your strengths. Be confident in your abilities and watch the world open its arms to you. Take a look at the list of things below. On it, you will find some things that you can do to help you get the job you need.

- Use the job descriptions you printed to build a good resume.
- Go online, look up resumes for the job you want and format your resume to match one you like.
- Get help if necessary.
- Research the job you want and learn the behaviors associated with that job.
- Practice saying five good things about yourself and make sure they are on your resume in one way or another.
- Talk to someone who is currently doing the job that you want to do.
- Determine if the job you want is actually the job you need.
- Think about your career path and how your next job fits into your future plans.

- Research how much companies pay for positions in the industry you work in.
- Find a different industry if you can't make enough money in the one you're in.

Loyalty

There's a time to be loyal and a time to clean out your desk and run. I learned that at an automotive factory, where I worked for many years. I put in my time. I was productive, efficient and effective. Everyday my team and I made the company money, but when it came time to close the factory, the owners didn't care about us as much as they did the money.

First, they hit us with layoffs, even though they knew beforehand that they had no intention of really laying us off. Every time someone got laid off, they got called back a couple of days later just to make sure no one could claim unemployment. After one day of work, they were all laid off again. It was the worst display of loyalty that I'd ever seen. I couldn't believe a company would stoop so low to save a buck.

People were struggling to pay their bills, while the company they'd been loyal to for years, were stabbing them in the back every chance it could get.

After struggling for months, everyone was finally let go. Suddenly, people who'd been loyal to the company for twenty plus years found themselves forced out. They ended up in a job market that cared nothing about the loyalty they showed to their previous employer. No one in the market wanted to take on the risk of hiring older employees, so many of them lost their homes and had to start over.

Just before the company closed, I walked off the job. The panic on the faces of the people was far too depressing for me. I just couldn't go to work every day and see those faces. People were hurting. They had families that were depending on them to make good decisions. They had kids that trusted them to make the right employment decisions, but they were loyal to the point that they were willing to go down with the ship.

I don't recommend you going down with the ship ever, unless you are going down with people who are going down with you. Even then, I'd advise you to think it through. Your decision to be loyal to a company that cares nothing about you, could be the reason why you are still in poverty. If it is, get out while you can. If the company is looking out for you, then great, but remember what I said. If it's not paying you what you're worth, then clean out your desk and get to stepping.

Education

Those who have an education have a little bit of an advantage, but an education doesn't necessarily guarantee success. I know plenty of people who have college degrees that still can't find their way out of poverty. That tells me that having an education is a good thing, but it's not the only thing. I'm not telling you to drop out of school, but what I'm saying is that a lack of education shouldn't stop you from reaching your goals. If you don't have a high school diploma or a college degree, then focus on the things that you do have, for example, creativity, drive, work ethic, and loyalty. The attributes that you do have can be the driving force behind your success.

There are many careers that don't require a degree and some of them pay pretty good money. You can make a good living as a sales professional, operator, inspector, manager or supervisor. With a little hard work, you can work your way to the top of almost any company, even the ones that require a degree. In the world of business, talent trumps all things, especially when it's accompanied by a positive attitude and a great work ethic. Think about that next time you skip over a job, just because it requires a degree.

Back to the Map

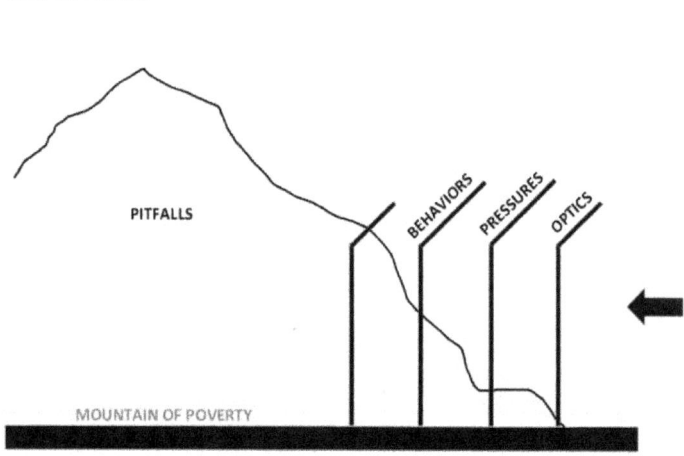

If I had to compare it to something, I would liken the beginning stages of your escape to the beginning stages of the Revolutionary War. Before the war began, there was a long period of uncertainty. There was a time when the thirteen colonies longed for independence but didn't know how to get it. All it took was a decade of small steps, some of which were never seen, heard or remembered. One step at a time the thirteen colonies worked their way towards freedom. It wasn't easy but they didn't give up. Armed with a new perspective, an unforgettable plan, a little bit of courage and a map, the colonists went to war for the world's greatest treasure. Their victory serves as a reminder of how important it is to be patient.

Like the thirteen colonies, you must be willing to stay the course until the time is right. Once you've armed yourself with a new perspective, a great plan, the same kind of courage and a map, you can do as the colonists did and take on the forces that stand between you and freedom. But before you do, you must know that a great understanding of the map is paramount.

The beauty of the map is that it's simple, but in its simplicity there's a tremendous amount of detail that is often missed. Details like length, width, height and depth might be seen by some, but overlooked by others. A closer look at the map can give you an idea of how long each category should take, but keep in mind that people are different. The amount of time it takes for you to change your optics might not be the same for someone else. You might be good at handling pressure, while others might just crumble under pressure. You might be quick to develop good behaviors, while others may have no idea what good behaviors are. Your plan needs to be your plan, so put together a good plan, using the map and make it your own.

Conclusion

I spent many nights thinking about how to end this book and every night I came up with the same answer. A book like this should never end. It should go on as long as poverty exist. Instead of ending it with a profound piece of knowledge, I decided to end it by encouraging you to go back to the beginning and reinforce what you've already learned. Learning the material is more important than ending this book with wise words.

Revisit the section on perception. Practice gratitude until it comes naturally. Confirm that you truly believe in yourself and eliminate any doubt that you can escape. With belief comes courage. Be courageous. Try some things you've never tried before. Talk to someone who has done what you're trying to do. Most important of all, eliminate the illusion that you are in this battle alone.

Acknowledgments

This book would not have been possible without the sacrifices of the many people who coached me throughout my career. My co-managers and sales teams inspired me to be the best that I could be and for that I'm eternally grateful. My daughter Adriana served as editor for this book and for her I have nothing but gratitude and respect. It was her first time playing the role of editor, but she took the bull by the horns and steered this book in the right direction.

To all of you who interviewed for this book, I appreciate you. Your stories are already helping me improve the lives of others. Your contribution to this book will change the lives of those who need this information the most; so, thank you. To the children of Covenant House Academy in Grand Rapid,

Michigan, thank you for sharing your struggles with me. I wish you off to a good start as you begin your lives in the world. Keep working. I love you, and I believe in you.

Notes

Preface

- As unique as your situation seems to be, someone has more than likely gone through it before.
- History is a great teacher, so your inspiration does not have to come from someone who's alive today. It can come from someone who lived long ago.
- Your breakthrough moment can happen at any time.

Introduction

- A thirteen percent chance is all you need to make your escape.
- People in the same or similar situation as yours have escaped before.
- Prison comes in many forms.
- You are not glued to your birthplace, sometimes you have to move.

The Map

- Knowing where you are in the process is important.
- Referring to your map gives you the best chance to escape. Knowing where you're going can give you the confidence you need to stay the course.

The Order

- The order is not optional. It should be followed. Doing things out of order will decrease your chances of escaping.
- Be patient with yourself and have confidence in your ability to escape.

The Revelation

- Beware of the illusion. Seeing things for what they really are is important.
- You already have the tools you need to escape.
- Control your emotions and don't panic when things get tough.

Perception

- Your escape depends on you having the right perception, so be willing to change it if necessary.
- You don't have to change who you are.
- Verify that you believe in yourself.

Pressures

- Your ability to deal with adversity will be the defining factor.
- Failure is inevitable, so embrace your failures and be prepared to fail even more in the future.
- Failure is another opportunity to grow.
- Know who's in your corner and eliminate those who are not.

Behaviors

- Your progress will be determined by what you do, so be prepared to do new things.
- Some things will need to be done differently.
- Meet new people, visit new places and be open to learning new things.
- Work hard, listen and overcome.
- See and recognize greatness.

Pitfalls

- Your decisions will determine how hard it will be for you to escape.
- The consequences of your decisions may be too much for you to bare.
- Your wants should not be more important than your needs.

References

Fontenot, Kayla, Jessica Semega and Melissa Kollar, U.S. Census Bureau, Current Population Reports, P60-263, *Income and Poverty in the United States: 2017*, U.S. Government Printing Office, Washington, DC, 2018

Biography.com Editors. (2016). Harry Houdini Biography. Retrieved from http://www.biography.com./people/harry-houdini-40056

U.S. Census Bureau, *Poverty: 2010 and 2011*, September, 2012

U.S. Bureau of Labor Statistics, *A Profile of the Working Poor*, 2010, January 2013

Stevens, Huff, H. *Transitions into & out of Poverty in the United States.* Volume 1, Number 1. Retrieved from https://poverty.ucdavis.edu/policy-brief/transitions-out-poverty-united-states

Bishaw, Alemayehu and Craig Benson. U.S. Census Bureau, Poverty: 2016 and 2017. Retrieved from http://www.census.gov/library/publications/2018/acs/acsbr17-02.html

To the teachers, educators and those who work in the education field:

So much of what you do go unnoticed, yet you continue to make a difference in the lives of those who have no one else. The kids who were born in poverty need you now more than ever. With so many things to distract them, it's a wonder that they still show up for school. A lot of kids show up only because you are there.

You are a big part of their lives, just as my favorite teacher, Mrs. Rhymes, was a big part of my life. If it wasn't for her, I don't know where I would be. It's people like you — teachers — that make the world a great place. Keep doing what you're doing and remember, you are on the front line of the battle; without you, we are in big trouble.

About the Author

Calvin Morris is a transformational leader that believes in helping others improve. He has experience in many different fields including sales, retail management, real estate, law enforcement, graphic design and manufacturing. Calvin believes in helping others because to him, success is not about how much money you make, it's about how many people you help. That's why he spends a lot of his time teaching others how to invest in themselves. He loves mentoring and helping others build online profiles, resumes, and growth strategies. Join him in his mission to help others break free from poverty. Reach out to someone that needs your help. Today is as good as any.

Connect with others who are trying to escape at: https://m.facebook.com/Escaping-Poverty-374387243405572. Once you've joined the conversation, you can invite as many people as you like, especially people who are trying to escape. You never know what you might learn from someone who has been through what you're going through or going through what you've been through. Find someone to help in the next 24 hours, and either buy that person a copy of the book or give him or her your copy. Pay it forward.

www.ingramcontent.com/pod-product-compliance
Lightning Source LLC
Chambersburg PA
CBHW071208070526
44584CB00019B/2961